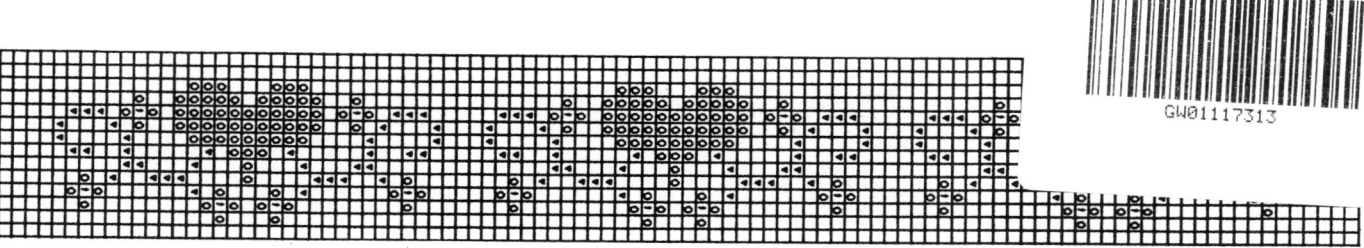

Traditional Floral Charted Designs for Borders and Bands

by Elizabeth Nyhan

DOVER PUBLICATIONS, INC.
New York

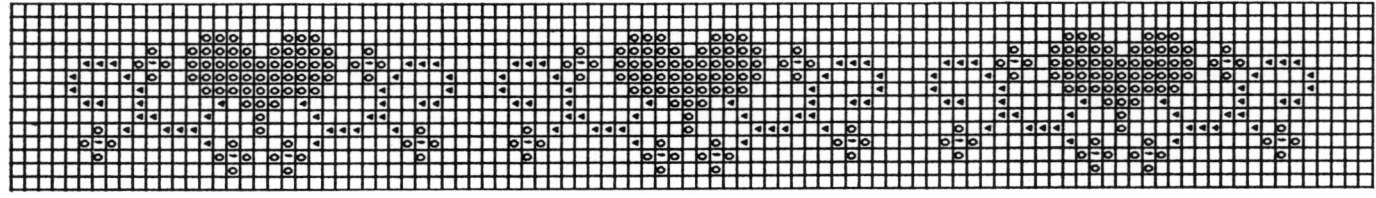

The colors used in the cover embroidery may vary from those listed in the color key for each design.

Copyright © 1991 by Elizabeth F. Nyhan.
All rights reserved under Pan American and International Copyright Conventions.

Published in Canada by General Publishing Company, Ltd., 30 Lesmill Road, Don Mills, Toronto, Ontario.
Published in the United Kingdom by Constable and Company, Ltd., 3 The Lanchesters, 162–164 Fulham Palace Road, London W6 9ER.

Traditional Floral Charted Designs for Borders and Bands is a new work, first published by Dover Publications, Inc., in 1991.

Manufactured in the United States of America
Dover Publications, Inc.
31 East 2nd Street, Mineola, N.Y. 11501

Library of Congress Cataloging-in-Publication Data

Nyhan, Elizabeth F.
Traditional floral charted designs for borders and bands / by Elizabeth Nyhan.
p.   cm. — (Dover needlework series)
ISBN 0-486-26696-6
1. Needlework—Patterns.   2. Decoration and ornament—Plant forms.
I. Title. II. Series.
TT753.N93   1991
746.44—dc20   90-28120
                              CIP

Introduction

The Bavarian Alps, located in southern Germany, are renowned for their beautiful mountains, friendly inns, quaint villages and townsfolk dressed in traditional costume.

The designs in this book are inspired by those found on decorative ribbons from the region. These fabric ribbons, ranging in width from ½" to 4", are used to decorate clothing and household items.

The basic folk costume worn by women in the Bavarian Alps, called a *dirndl*, includes a print dress and matching apron over a white blouse with puffed sleeves. Fancier versions might feature silk material, lace and eyelet embellishment on the blouse or apron, fancy buttons or an elaborate petticoat.

The men's traditional costume of leather shorts or knee-length pants, called *lederhosen*, is usually accompanied by leather suspenders.

Both men and women wear suits, jackets and coats of *loden*, a specially processed, waterproof wool. Suits and jackets are seen in a number of colors, but dark green is the traditional color for loden coats.

Because the designs are taken from ribbons, they are *repeat* patterns, that is, the basic design unit is repeated over and over until the desired length is reached. Such designs can be used alone for belts, bellpulls, luggage straps, etc., or as a finishing touch for another design. All of the designs are shown with a border, which can be omitted if you wish. The width of each design, with and without the border, the design length and the repeat length are given with each chart. These measurements are given in *squares*; the measurement in inches depends, of course, on how many threads per inch there are in your fabric. The design length is the number of squares needed to center a single repeat on the fabric, having each side of the repeat symmetrical. The repeat length tells you how many squares each *additional* repeat will need.

It is best to begin a repeat pattern in the center and work out so that the design is balanced. Sometimes, there is more than one possible center of a design. For example, the center can fall between two repeats or at the center of the repeat itself.

It is very easy to design a corner for your border with the aid of a small rectangular mirror and some graph paper. Holding the mirror on edge, place it across the chart at a 45° angle. The design will be reflected in the mirror at a right angle and a perfect corner will be formed. Move the mirror along the chart until you find a corner design that you like, then copy it onto the graph paper.

Counted Cross-stitch

MATERIALS

1. **Needles.** A small blunt tapestry needle, No. 24 or No. 26.

2. **Fabric.** Evenweave linen, cotton, wool or synthetic fabrics all work well. The most popular fabrics are aida cloth, linen and hardanger cloth. Cotton aida is most commonly available in 18 threads-per-inch, 14 threads-per-inch and 11 threads-per-inch (14-count is the most popular size). Evenweave linen comes in a variety of threads-per-inch. To work cross-stitch on linen involves a slightly different technique (see page 5). Thirty thread-per-inch linen will result in a stitch about the same size as 14-count aida. Hardanger cloth has 22 threads to the inch and is available in cotton or linen. The amount of fabric needed depends on the size of the cross-stitch design. To determine yardage, divide the number of stitches in the design by the thread-count of the fabric. For example: If a design 112 squares wide by 140 squares deep is worked on a 14-count fabric, divide 112 by 14 (=8), and 140 by 14 (=10). The design will measure 8" × 10". The same design worked on 22-count fabric measures about 5" × 6½".

3. **Threads and Yarns.** Six-strand embroidery floss, crewel wool, Danish Flower Thread, pearl cotton or metallic threads all work well for cross-stitch. DMC Embroidery Floss has been used to color-code the patterns in this volume. Crewel wool works well on evenweave wool fabric. Danish Flower Thread is a thicker thread with a matte finish, one strand equaling two of embroidery floss.

4. **Embroidery Hoop.** A wooden or plastic 4", 5" or 6" round or oval hoop with a screw-type tension adjuster works best for cross-stitch.

5. **Scissors.** A pair of sharp embroidery scissors is essential to all embroidery.

PREPARING TO WORK

To prevent raveling, either whip stitch or machine-stitch the outer edges of the fabric.

Locate the exact center of the chart. Establish the center of the fabric by folding it in half first vertically, then horizontally. The center stitch of the chart falls where the creases of the fabric meet. Mark the fabric center with a basting thread.

It is best to begin cross-stitch at the top of the design. To establish the top, count the squares up from the center of the chart, and the corresponding number of holes up from the center of the fabric.

Place the fabric tautly in the embroidery hoop, for tension makes it easier to push the needle through the holes without piercing the fibers. While working continue to retighten the fabric as necessary.

When working with multiple strands (such as embroidery floss) always separate (strand) the thread before beginning to stitch. This one small step allows for better coverage of the fabric. When you need more than one thread in the needle, use separate strands and do not double the thread. (For example: If you need four strands, use four separated strands.) Thread has a nap (just as fabrics do) and can be felt to be smoother in one direction than the other. Always work with the nap (the smooth side) pointing down.

For 14-count aida and 30-count linen, work with two strands of six-strand floss. For more texture, use more thread; for a flatter look, use less thread.

EMBROIDERY

To begin, fasten the thread with a waste knot and hold a short length of thread on the underside of the work, anchoring it with the first few stitches *(Diagram 1)*. When the thread end is securely in place, clip the knot.

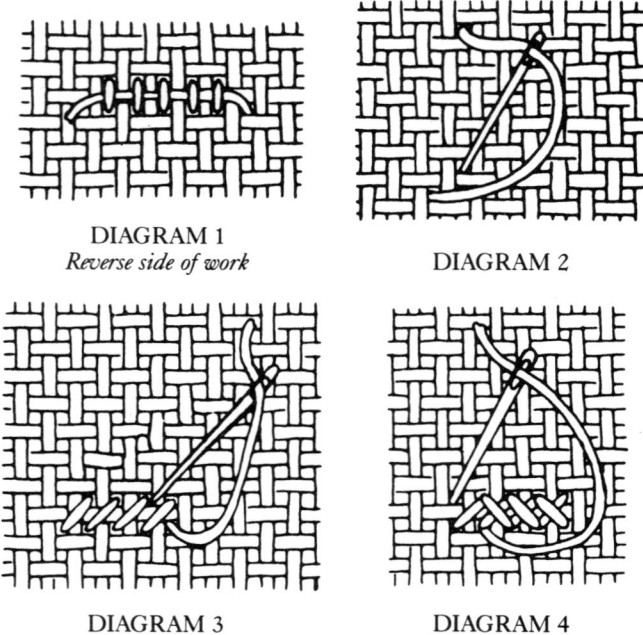

DIAGRAM 1
Reverse side of work

DIAGRAM 2

DIAGRAM 3

DIAGRAM 4

To stitch, push the needle up through a hole in the fabric, cross the thread intersection (or square) on a left-to-right diagonal *(Diagram 2)*. Half the stitch is now completed.

Next, cross back, right to left, forming an X *(Diagram 3)*.

Work all the same color stitches on one row, then cross back, completing the X's *(Diagram 4)*.

Some needleworkers prefer to cross each stitch as they come to it. This method also works, but be sure all of the top stitches are slanted in the same direction. Isolated stitches must be crossed as they are worked. Vertical stitches are crossed as shown in *Diagram 5*.

DIAGRAM 5

At the top, work horizontal rows of a single color, left to right. This method allows you to go from an unoccupied space to an occupied space (working from an empty hole to a filled one), making ruffling of the floss less likely. Holes are used more than once, and all stitches "hold hands" unless a space is indicated on the chart. Hold the work upright throughout (do not turn as with many needlepoint stitches).

When carrying the thread from one area to another, run the needle under a few stitches on the wrong side. Do not carry thread across an open expanse of fabric as it will be visible from the front when the project is completed.

To end a color, weave in and out of the underside of the stitches, making a scallop stitch or two for extra security *(Diagram 6)*. When possible, end in the same direction in which you were working, jumping up a row if necessary *(Diagram 7)*. This prevents holes caused by stitches being pulled in two directions. Trim the thread ends closely and do not leave any tails or knots as they will show through the fabric when the work is completed.

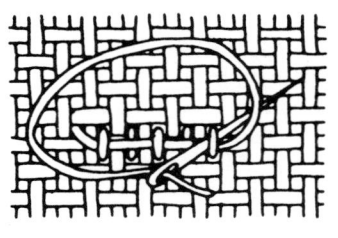 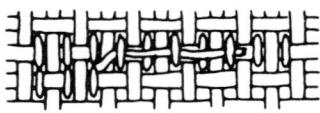

DIAGRAM 6
Reverse side of work

DIAGRAM 7
Reverse side of work

DIAGRAM 8

A number of other counted-thread stitches can be used in cross-stitch. Backstitch *(Diagram 8)* is used for outlines, face details and the like. It is worked from hole to hole, and may be stitched as a vertical, horizontal or diagonal line.

DIAGRAM 9

Straight stitch is worked from side to side over several threads *(Diagram 9)* and affords solid coverage.

DIAGRAM 10

Embroidery on Linen. Working on linen requires a slightly different technique. While evenweave linen is remarkably regular, there are always a few thick or thin threads. To keep the stitches even, cross-stitch is worked over two threads in each direction *(Diagram 10)*.

As you are working over more threads, linen affords a greater variation in stitches. A half-stitch can slant in either direction and is uncrossed. A three-quarters stitch is shown in *Diagram 11*.

DIAGRAM 11

Diagram 12 shows the backstitch worked on linen.

DIAGRAM 12

Embroidery on Gingham. Gingham and other checked fabrics can be used for cross-stitch. Using the fabric as a guide, work the stitches from corner to corner of each check.

Embroidery on Uneven-Weave Fabrics. If you wish to work cross-stitch on an uneven-weave fabric, baste a lightweight Penelope needlepoint canvas to the material. The design can then be stitched by working the cross-stitch over the double mesh of the canvas. When working in this manner, take care not to catch the threads of the canvas in the embroidery. After the cross-stitch is completed, remove the basting threads. With tweezers, remove first the vertical threads, one strand at a time, of the needlepoint canvas, then the horizontal threads.

Needlepoint

One of the most common methods for working needlepoint is from a charted design. By simply viewing each square of a chart as a stitch on the canvas, the patterns quickly and easily translate from one technique to another.

MATERIALS

1. **Needles.** A blunt tapestry needle with a rounded tip and an elongated eye. The needle must clear the hole of the canvas without spreading the threads. For No. 10 canvas, a No. 18 needle works best.

2. **Canvas.** There are two distinct types of needlepoint canvas: single-mesh (mono canvas) and double-mesh (Penelope canvas). Single-mesh canvas, the more common of the two, is easier on the eyes as the spaces are slightly larger. Double-mesh canvas has two horizontal and two vertical threads forming each mesh. The latter is a very stable canvas on which the threads stay securely in place as the work progresses. Canvas is available in many sizes, from 5 mesh-per-inch to 18 mesh-per-inch, and even smaller. The number of mesh-per-inch will, of course, determine the dimensions of the finished needlepoint project. A 60 square × 120 square chart will measure 12″ × 24″ on 5 mesh-to-the-inch canvas, 5″ × 10″ on 12 mesh-to-the-inch canvas. The most common canvas size is 10 to the inch.

3. **Yarns.** Persian, crewel and tapestry yarns all work well on needlepoint canvas.

PREPARING TO WORK

Allow 1″ to 1½″ blank canvas all around. Bind the raw edges of the canvas with masking tape or machine-stitched double-fold bias tape.

There are few hard-and-fast rules on where to begin the design. It is best to complete the main motif, then fill the background as the last step.

For any guidelines you wish to draw on the canvas, take care that your marking medium is waterproof. Nonsoluble inks, acrylic paints thinned with water so as not to clog the mesh, and waterproof felt-tip pens all work well. If unsure, experiment on a scrap of canvas.

When working with multiple strands (such as Persian yarn) always separate (strand) the yarn before beginning to stitch. This one small step allows for better coverage of the canvas. When you need more than one piece of yarn in the needle, use separate strands and do not double the yarn. For example: If you need two strands of 3-ply Persian yarn, use two separated strands. Yarn has a nap (just as fabrics do) and can be felt to be smoother in one direction than the other. Always work with the nap (the smooth side) pointing down.

For 5 mesh-to-the-inch canvas, use six strands of 3-ply yarn; for 10 mesh-to-the-inch canvas, use three strands of 3-ply yarn.

STITCHING

Cut yarn lengths 18″ long. Begin needlepoint by holding about 1″ of loose yarn on the wrong side of the work and working the first several stitches over the loose end to secure it. To end a piece of yarn, run it under several completed stitches on the wrong side of the work.

There are hundreds of needlepoint stitch variations, but tent stitch is universally considered to be *the* needlepoint stitch. The most familiar versions of tent stitch are half-cross stitch, continental stitch and basket-weave stitch.

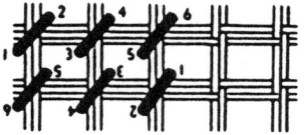   

DIAGRAM 13   DIAGRAM 14

Half-cross stitch *(Diagram 13)* is worked from left to right. The canvas is then turned around and the return row is again stitched from left to right. Holding the needle vertically, bring it to the front of the canvas through the hole that will be the bottom of the first stitch. Keep the stitches loose for minimum distortion and good coverage. Half-cross stitch is best worked on a double-mesh canvas.

Continental stitch *(Diagram 14)* begins in the upper right-hand corner and is worked from right to left. The needle is slanted and always brought out a mesh ahead. The resulting stitch appears as a half-cross stitch on the front and as a slanting stitch on the back. When the row is complete, turn the canvas around to work the return row, continuing to stitch from right to left.

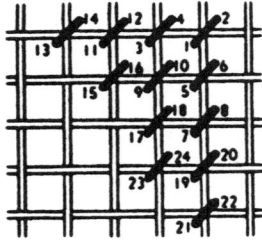

DIAGRAM 15

Basket-weave stitch *(Diagram 15)* begins in the upper right-hand corner with four continental stitches (two stitches worked horizontally across the top and two placed directly below the first stitch). Work diagonal rows, the first slanting up and across the canvas from right to left, and the next down and across from left to right. Moving down the canvas from left to right, the needle is in a vertical position; working in the opposite direction, the needle is horizontal. The rows interlock, creating a basket-weave pattern on the wrong side. If the stitch is not done properly, a faint ridge will show where the pattern was interrupted. On basket-weave stitch, always stop working in the middle of a row, rather than at the end, so that you will know in which direction you were working.

Knitting

Charted designs can be worked into stockinette stitch as you are knitting, or they can be embroidered with duplicate stitch when the knitting is complete. For the former, wind the different colors of yarn on bobbins and work in the same manner as in Fair Isle knitting. A few quick Fair Isle tips: (1) Always bring up the new color yarn from under the dropped color to prevent holes. (2) Carry the color not in use loosely across the wrong side of the work, but not more than three or four stitches without twisting the yarns. If a color is not in use for more than seven or eight stitches, it is usually best to drop that color yarn and rejoin a new bobbin when the color is again needed.

Crochet

There are a number of ways in which charts can be used for crochet. Among them are:

SINGLE CROCHET

Single crochet is often seen worked in multiple colors. When changing colors, always pick up the new color for the last yarn-over of the old color. The color not in use can be carried loosely across the back of the work for a few stitches, or you can work the single crochet over the unused color. The latter method makes for a neater appearance on the wrong side, but sometimes the old color peeks through the stitches. This method can also be applied to half-double crochet and double crochet, but keep in mind that the longer stitches will distort the design.

FILET CROCHET

This technique is nearly always worked from charts and uses only one color thread. The result is a solid-color piece with the design filled in and the background left as an open mesh. Care must be taken in selecting the design, as the longer stitch causes distortion.

AFGHAN CROCHET

The most common method here is cross-stitch worked over the afghan stitch. Complete the afghan crochet project. Then, following the chart for color placement, work cross-stitch over the squares of crochet.

Other Charted Methods

Latch hook, Assisi embroidery, beading, cross-stitch on needlepoint canvas (a European favorite) and lace net embroidery are among the other needlework methods worked from charts.

	DMC #	
⊙	326	very deep rose
■	469	avocado green
▲	899	medium rose

Width with border: 73 squares
Width without border: 53 squares
Design length: 95 squares
Repeat length: 76 squares

▲ DMC #

- ■ 311 medium navy blue
- ◙ 334 medium marine blue
-] 775 light baby blue

Width with border: 31 squares
Width without border: 19 squares
Design length: 69 squares
Repeat length: 69 squares

▲ DMC #

- ■ 3346 hunter green
- ◙ 3350 very dark dusty rose
- ▼ 3354 light dusty rose

Width with border: 33 squares
Width without border: 25 squares
Design length: 33 squares
Repeat length: 36 squares

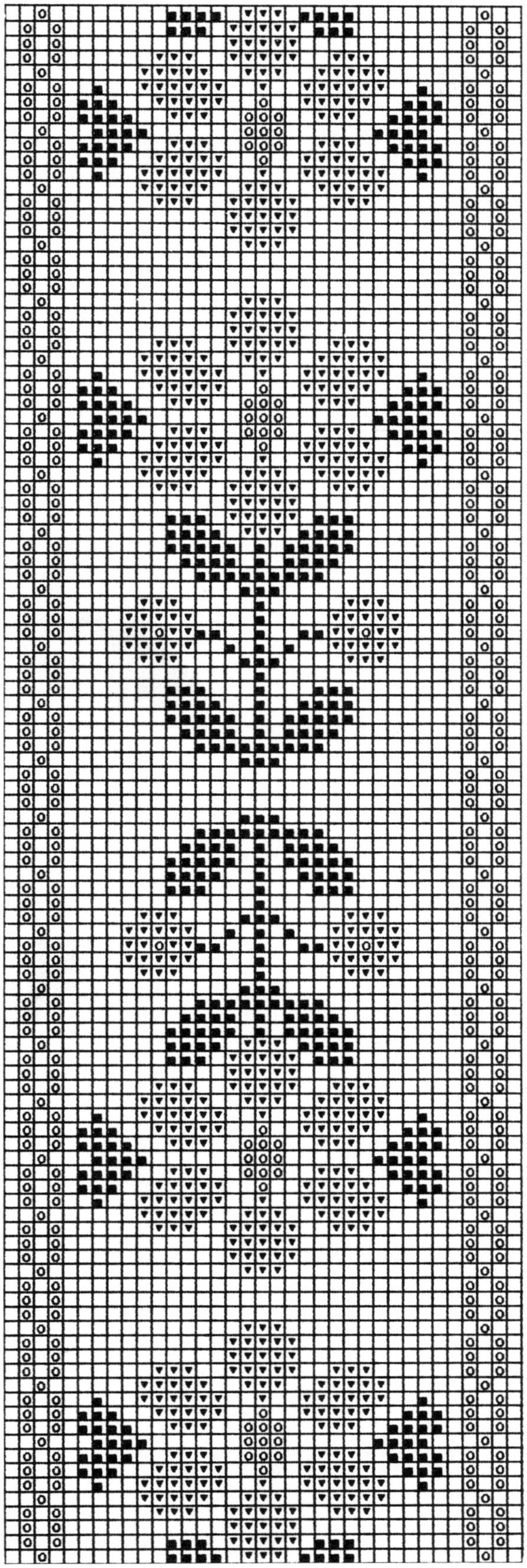

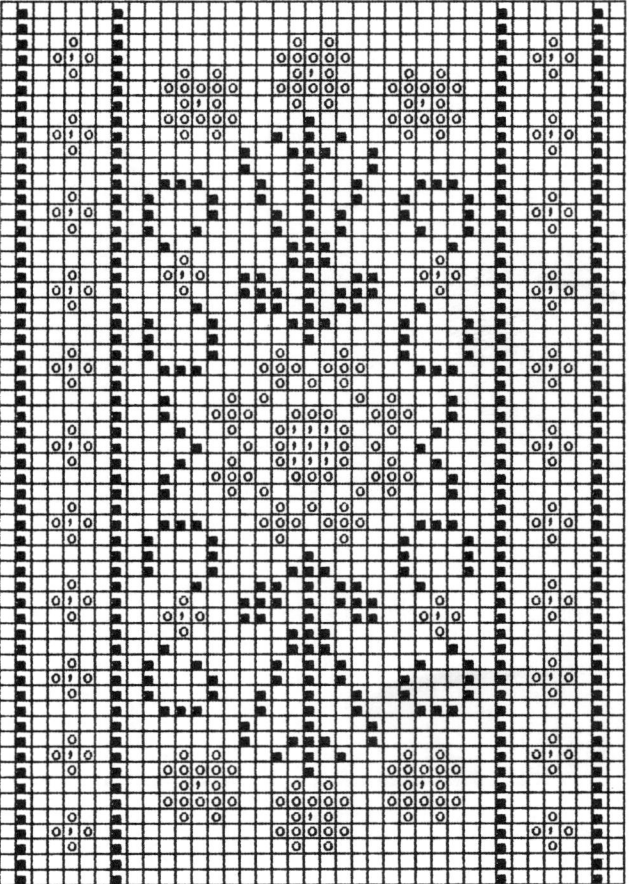

▲   *DMC #*

☐   826   medium blue
☐   828   very pale blue
■   954   Nile green

Width with border: 37 squares
Width without border: 21 squares
Design length: 53 squares
Repeat length: 53 squares

◄   *DMC #*

■   3346   hunter green
☐   3350   very dark dusty rose
▼   3354   light dusty rose

Width with border: 33 squares
Width without border: 25 squares
Design length: 69 squares
Repeat length: 72 squares

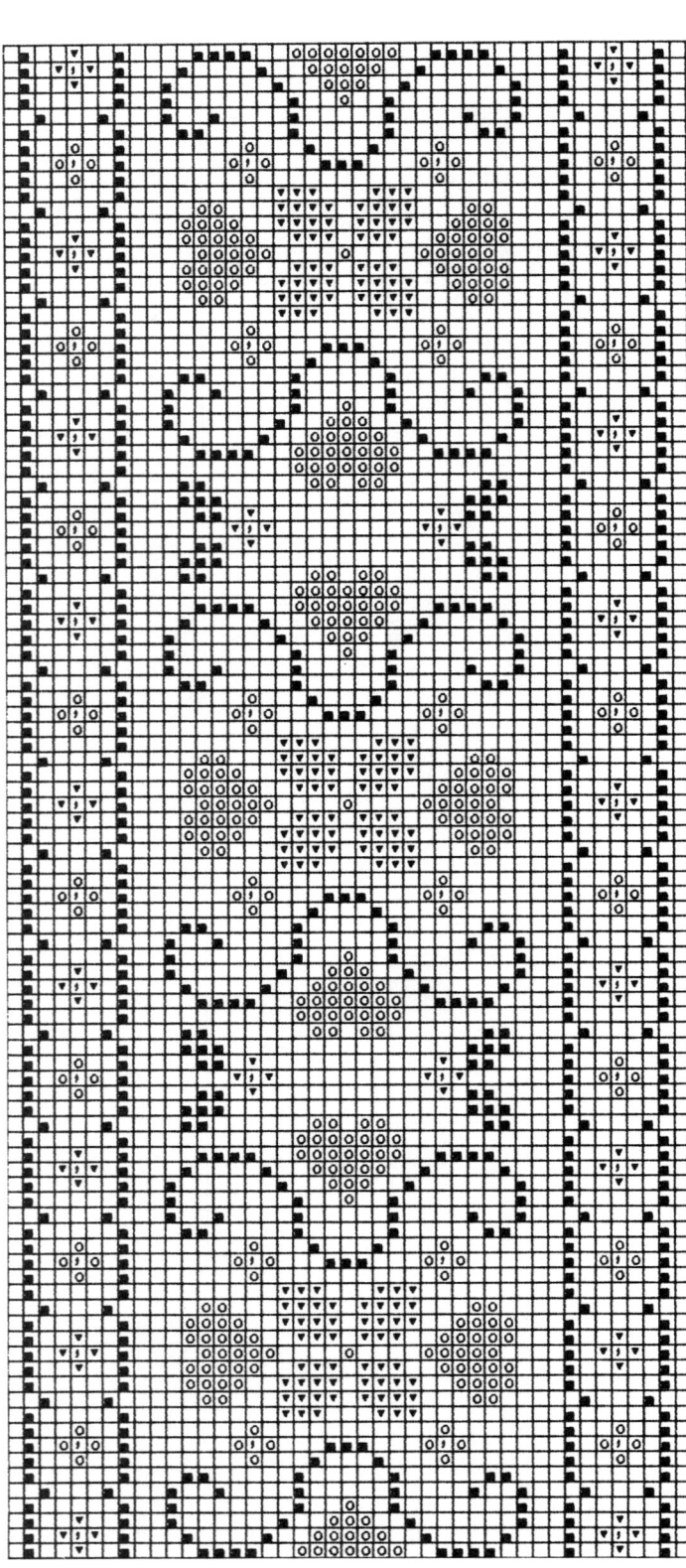

DMC #		
■	987	medium forest green
ꜛ	3078	very light golden yellow
▼	3350	very dark dusty rose
o	3354	light dusty rose

Width with border: 41 squares
Width without border: 23 squares
Design length: 43 squares
Repeat length: 36 squares

DMC #		
■	326	very deep rose
ꜛ	727	very light topaz
▶	987	medium forest green
o	3326	light rose

Width with border: 53 squares
Width without border: 39 squares
Design length: 39 squares
Repeat length: 44 squares

DMC #		
o	666	bright Christmas red
■	798	dark Delft blue

Width with border: 74 squares
Width without border: 52 squares
Design length: 45 squares
Repeat length: 48 squares

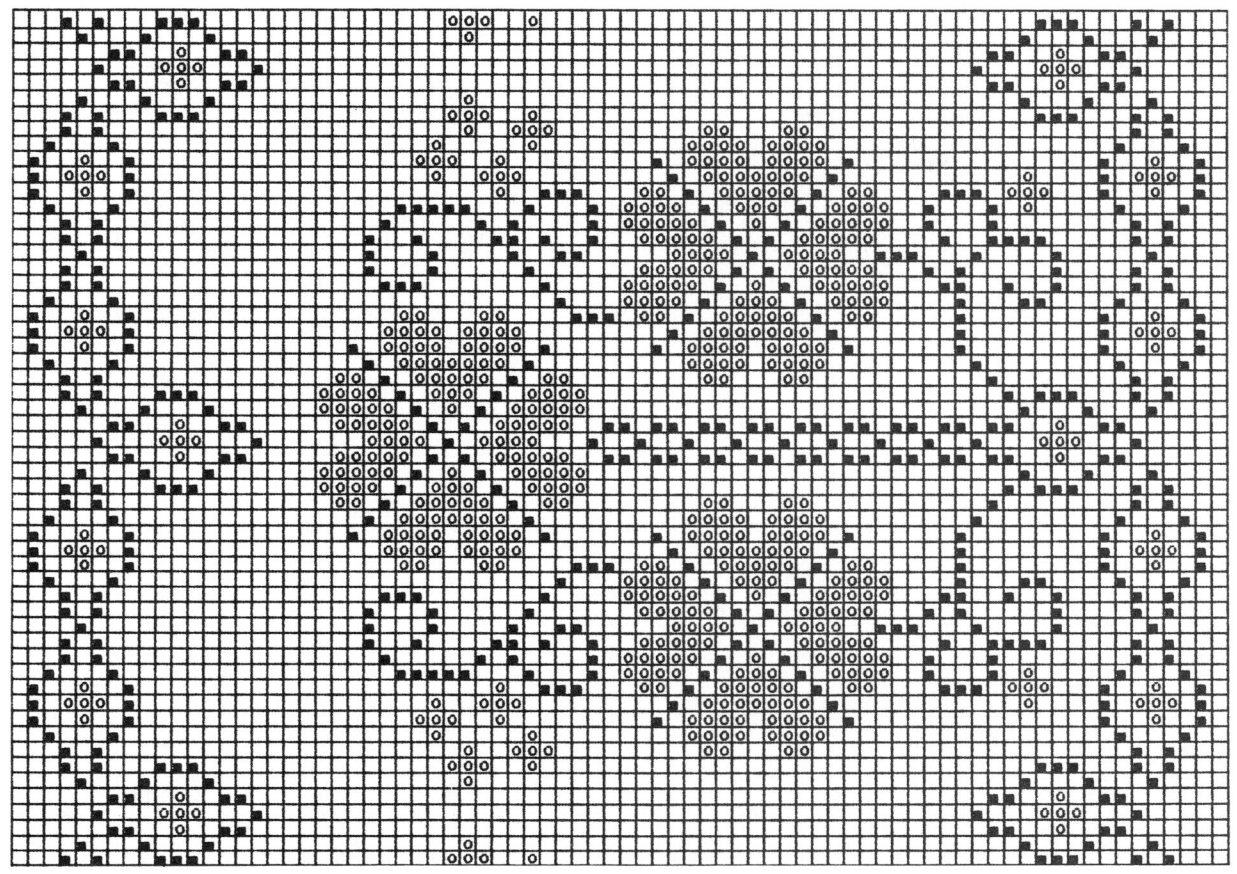

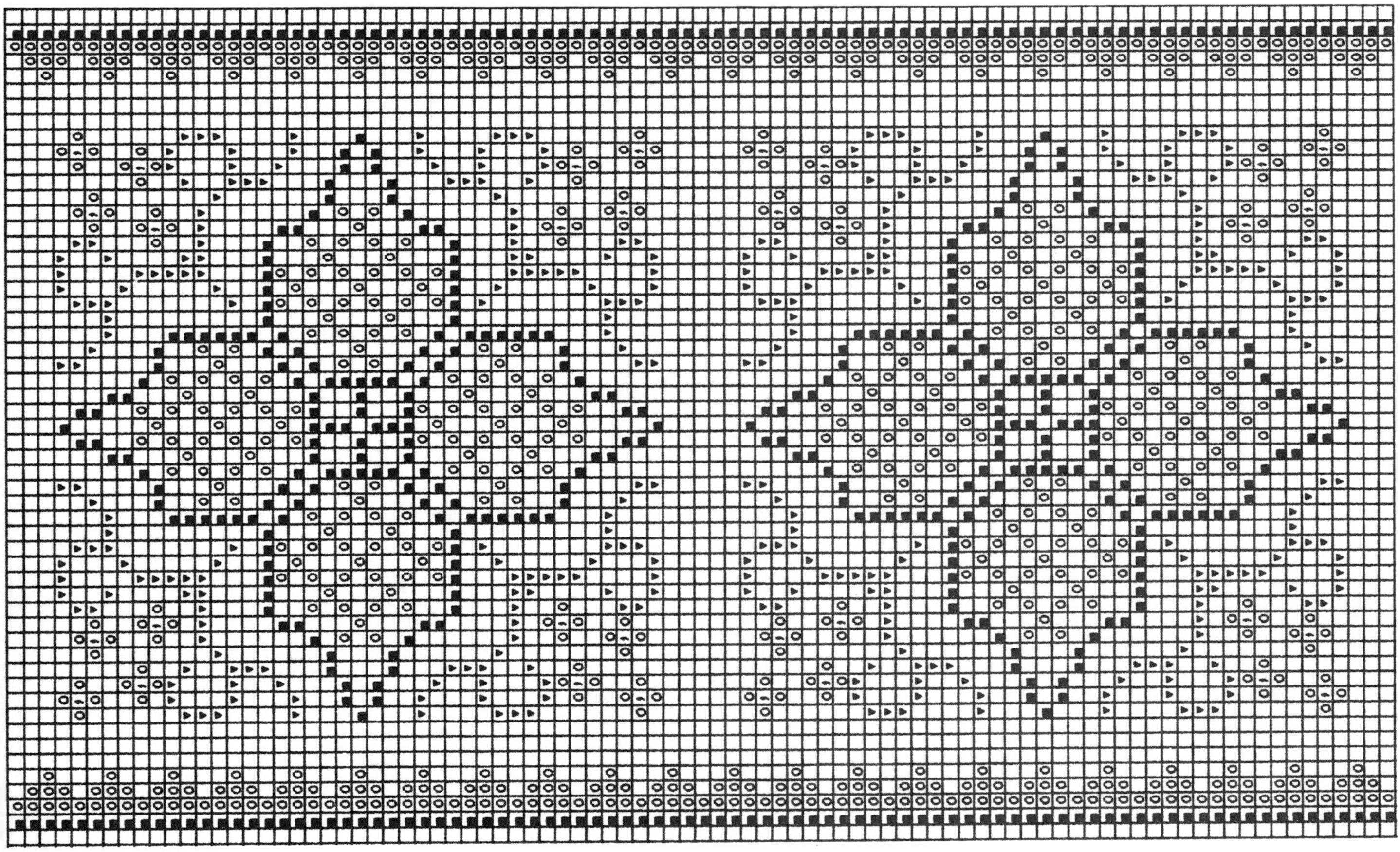

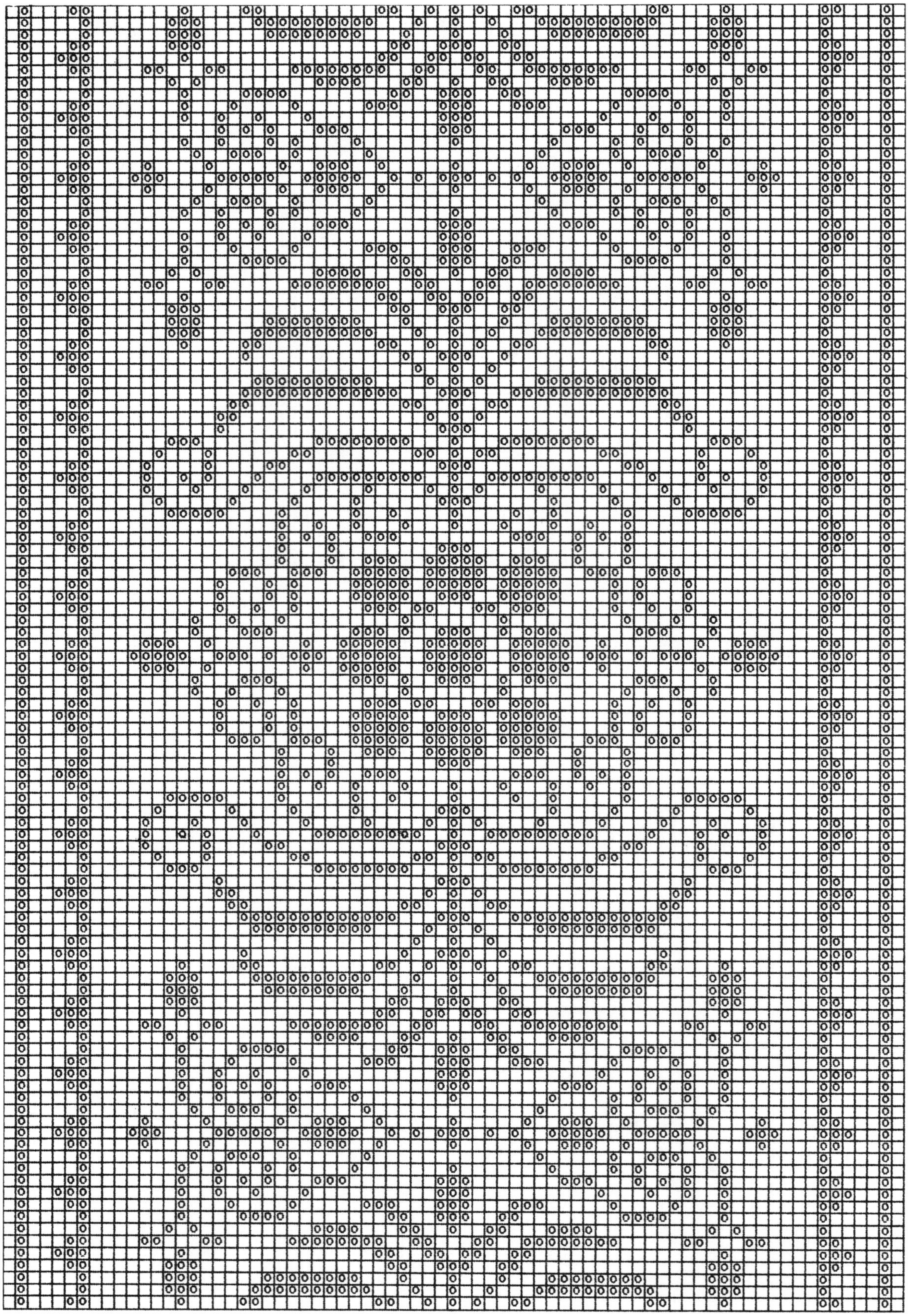

◄	DMC #	
◙	347	dark salmon

Width with border: 71 squares
Width without border: 53 squares
Design length: 109 squares
Repeat length: 80 squares

▲	DMC #	
◙	309	deep rose
■	319	very dark pistachio green
℩	776	medium pink

Width with border: 57 squares
Width without border: 45 squares
Design length: 89 squares
Repeat length: 68 squares

▲	DMC #	
▼	309	deep rose
■	319	very dark pistachio green
o	3326	light rose

Width with border: 51 squares
Width without border: 31 squares
Design length: 49 squares
Repeat length: 49 squares

▼	DMC #	
┇		white
▼	666	bright Christmas red
o	796	dark royal blue

Width with border: 61 squares
Width without border: 49 squares
Design length: 47 squares
Repeat length: 47 squares

	DMC #	
○	3345	dark hunter green
▼	3348	light yellow green

Width with border: 45 squares
Width without border: 31 squares
Design length: 43 squares
Repeat length: 36 squares

	DMC #	
○	825	dark blue
▼	828	very pale blue
■	988	forest green
⌐	3078	very light golden yellow

Width with border: 43 squares
Width without border: 19 squares
Design length: 37 squares
Repeat length: 37 squares

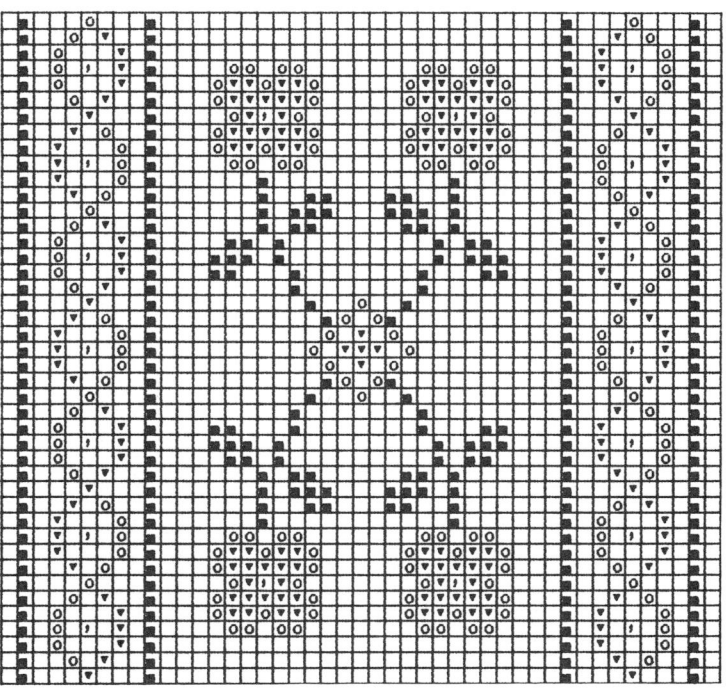

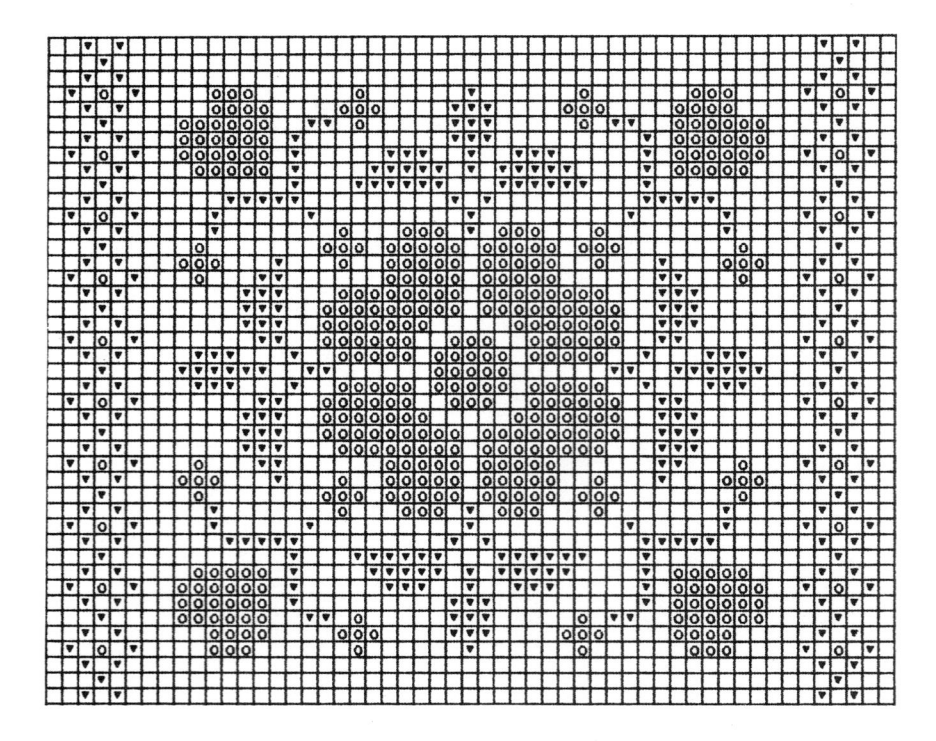

◄
	DMC #	
◐	962	medium dusty rose
▼	988	forest green

Width with border: 51 squares
Width without border: 37 squares
Design length: 37 squares
Repeat length: 37 squares

►
	DMC #	
■	326	very deep rose
1	818	baby pink
◐	3326	light rose

Width with border: 51 squares
Width without border: 37 squares
Design length: 37 squares
Repeat length: 37 squares

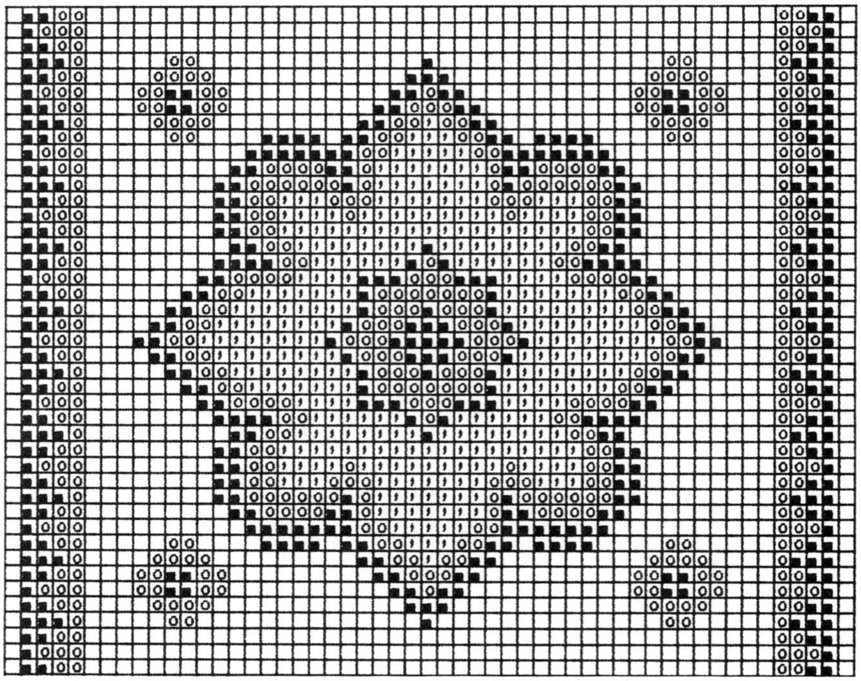

	DMC #		
◉	666	bright Christmas red
◼	699	Christmas green
▼	796	dark royal blue

Width with border: 61 squares
Width without border: 47 squares
Design length: 83 squares
Repeat length: 83 squares

▲

	DMC #	
▼	326	very deep rose
○	899	medium rose
■	987	medium forest green

Width with border: 37 squares
Width without border: 27 squares
Design length: 115 squares
Repeat length: 115 squares

▶

	DMC #	
○	973	bright canary yellow
■	3345	dark hunter green
1	740	tangerine

Width with border: 34 squares
Width without border: 25 squares
Design length: 40 squares
Repeat length: 40 squares

DMC #		light navy blue
312		light baby blue
775		very dark parrot green
904		
	or	
961		dark dusty rose
963		very light dusty rose

Width with border: 45 squares
Width without border: 27 squares
Design length: 27 squares
Repeat length: 32

	DMC #	
◉	347	dark salmon
■	838	very dark beige brown
▶	842	very light beige brown

Width with border: 57 squares
Width without border: 41 squares
Design length: 75 squares
Repeat length: 75 squares

	DMC #	
○	666	bright Christmas red
◀	726	light topaz
■	797	royal blue

Width with border: 63 squares
Width without border: 43 squares
Design length: 75 squares
Repeat length: 75 squares

DMC #

◘	312	light navy blue
▼	775	light baby blue
■	904	very dark parrot green

or

◘	961	dark dusty rose
▼	963	very light dusty rose

Width with border: 45 squares
Width without border: 27 squares
Design length: 51 squares
Repeat length: 32 squares

DMC #

■ 347 dark salmon
◉ 838 very dark beige brown

Width with border: 45 squares
Width without border: 35 squares
Design length: 57 squares
Repeat length: 36 squares

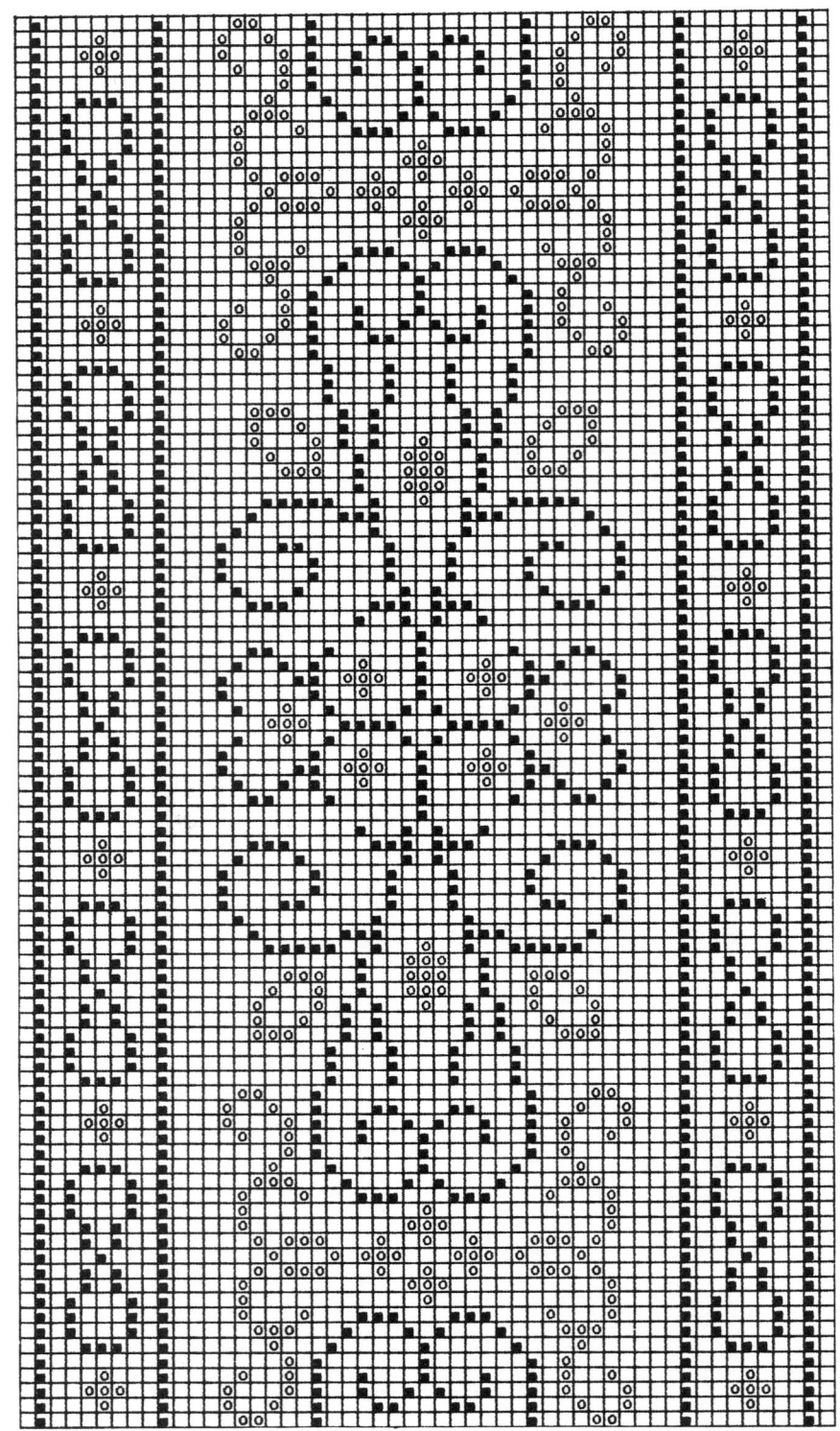

	DMC #	
○	973	bright canary yellow
■	3345	dark hunter green

Width with border: 51 squares
Width without border: 27 squares
Design length: 95 squares
Repeat length: 72 squares

	DMC #	
o	972	yellow orange
♪	973	bright canary yellow
■	3346	hunter green

Width with border: 57 squares
Width without border: 37 squares
Design length: 53 squares
Repeat length: 42 squares

DMC #
▲ 826 medium blue
⏺ 828 very pale blue

Width with border: 41 squares
Width without border: 17 squares
Design length: 105 squares
Repeat length: 105 squares

DMC #
◉ 827   very light blue

Width with border: 47 squares
Width without border: 27 squares
Design length: 61 squares
Repeat length: 42 squares

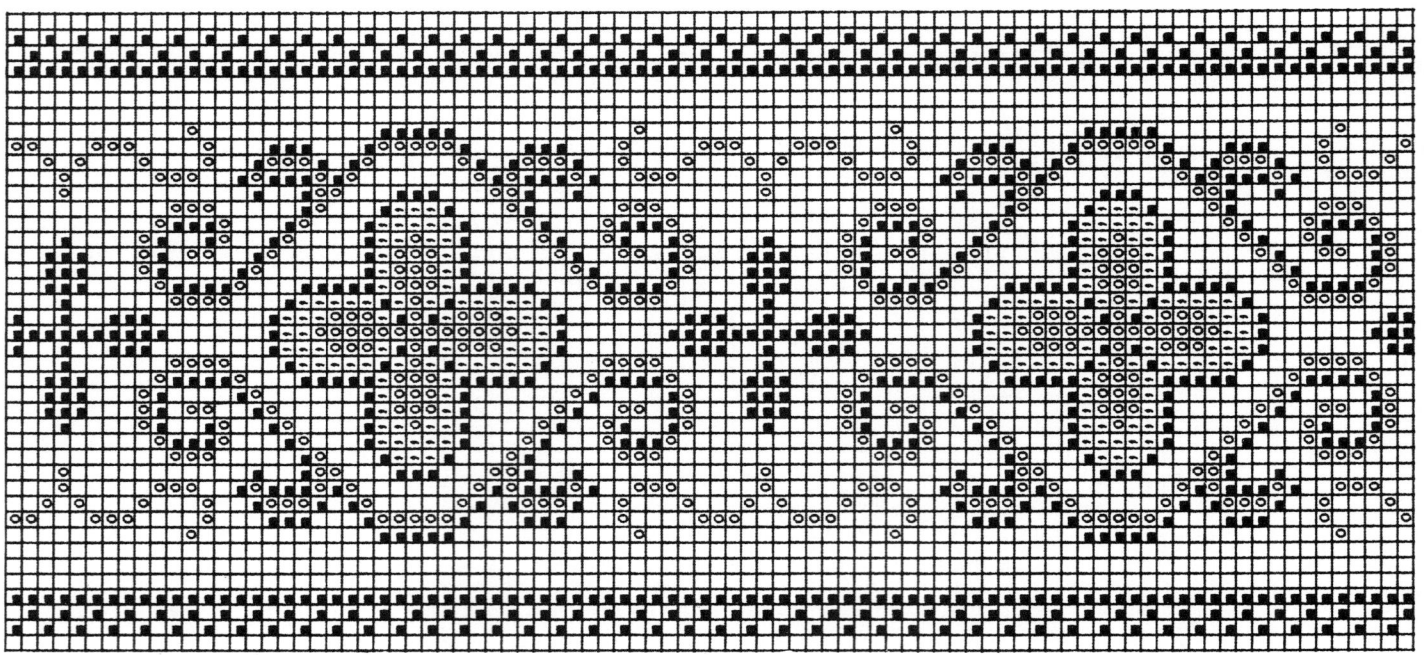

▲

	DMC #	
◉	334	medium marine blue
■	336	navy blue
−	775	light baby blue

Width with border: 39 squares
Width without border: 27 squares
Design length: 63 squares
Repeat length: 44 squares

▼

	DMC #	
◉	813	light blue
◀	825	dark blue

Width with border: 41 squares
Width without border: 25 squares
Design length: 25 squares
Repeat length: 24

▲	DMC #	
−	326	very deep rose
○	367	dark pistachio green
▶	899	medium rose

Width with border: 17 squares
Width without border: 9 squares
Design length: 31 squares
Repeat length: 28 squares

▼	DMC #	
◀	666	bright Christmas red
■	699	Christmas green
○	796	dark royal blue

Width with border: 47 squares
Width without border: 32 squares
Design length: 83 squares
Repeat length: 83 squares

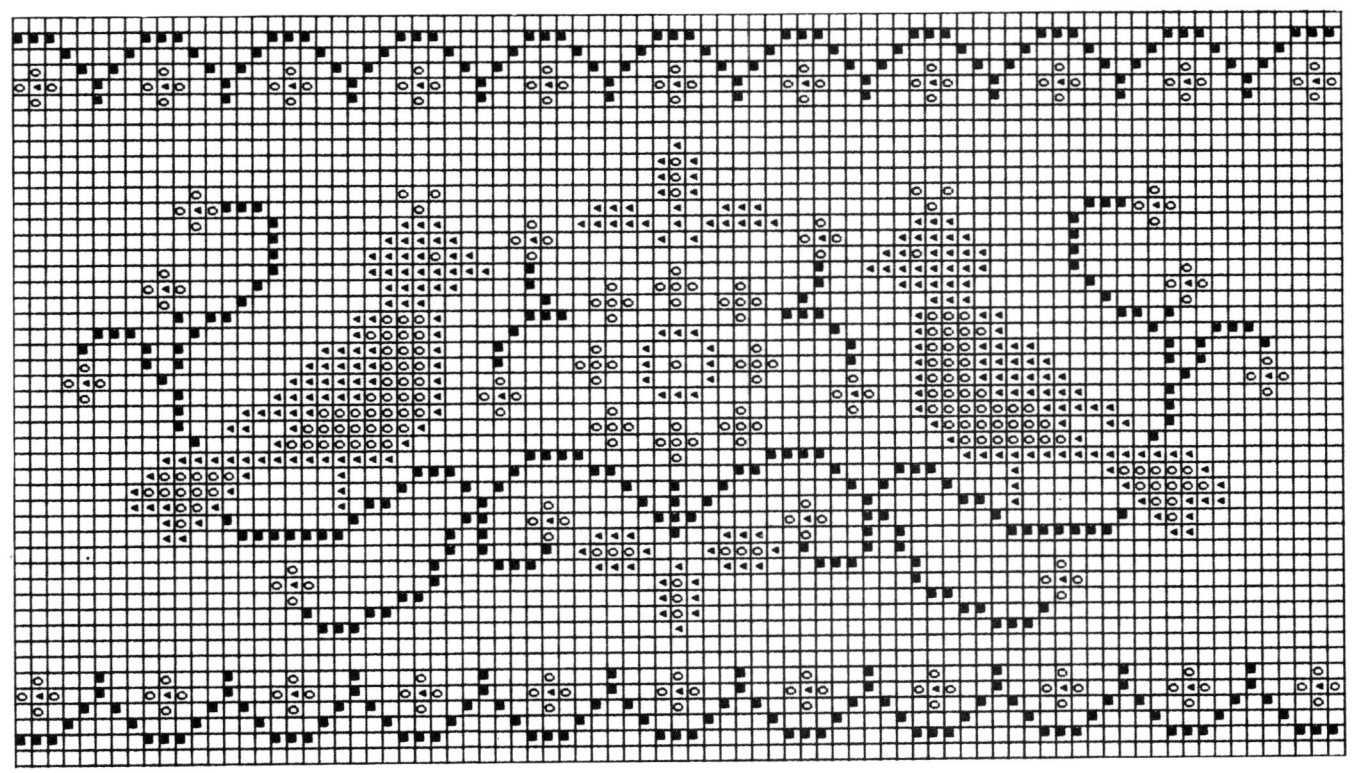

	DMC #		
▶	601	dark cranberry	Width with border: 57 squares
○	602	medium cranberry	Width without border: 35 squares
■	605	very light cranberry	Design length: 83 squares
⌐	955	light Nile green	Repeat length: 60 squares

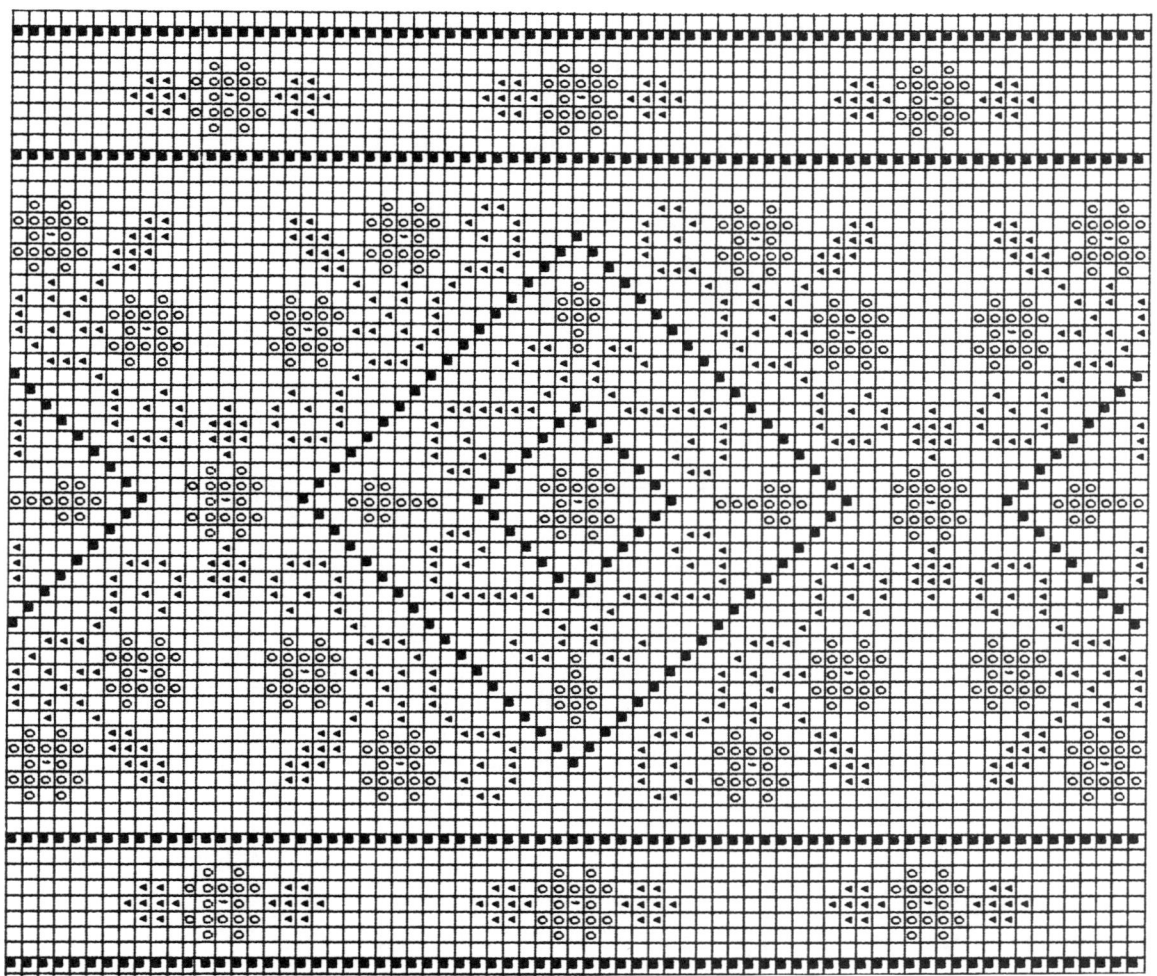

	DMC #		
■	309	deep rose	Width with border: 61 squares
⊡	819	light baby pink	Width without border: 39 squares
◀	987	medium forest green	Design length: 49 squares
◯	3326	light rose	Repeat length: 44 squares

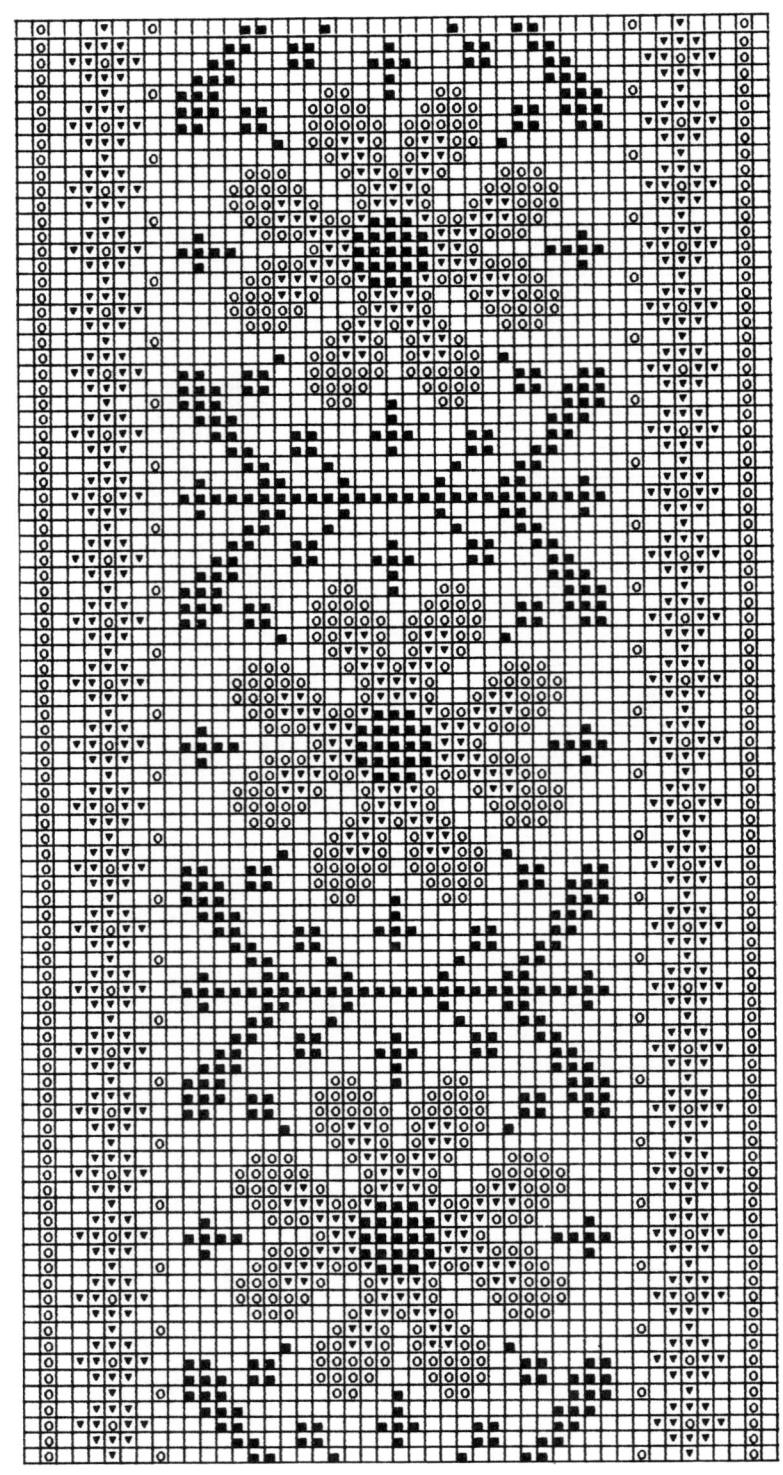

	DMC #		
○	312	light navy blue	Width with border: 45 squares
▼	775	light baby blue	Width without border: 27 squares
■	904	very dark parrot green	Design length: 109 squares
		or	Repeat length: 109 squares
○	961	dark dusty rose	
▼	963	very light dusty rose	

	DMC #	
o	772	very light loden green
▼	3362	dark loden green

Width with border: 53 squares
Width without border: 31 squares
Design length: 89 squares
Repeat length: 89 squares

	DMC #	
■	319	very dark pistachio green
O	326	very deep rose
▼	818	baby pink
꜌	899	medium rose

Width with border: 57 squares
Width without border: 45 squares
Design length: 119 squares
Repeat length: 98 squares

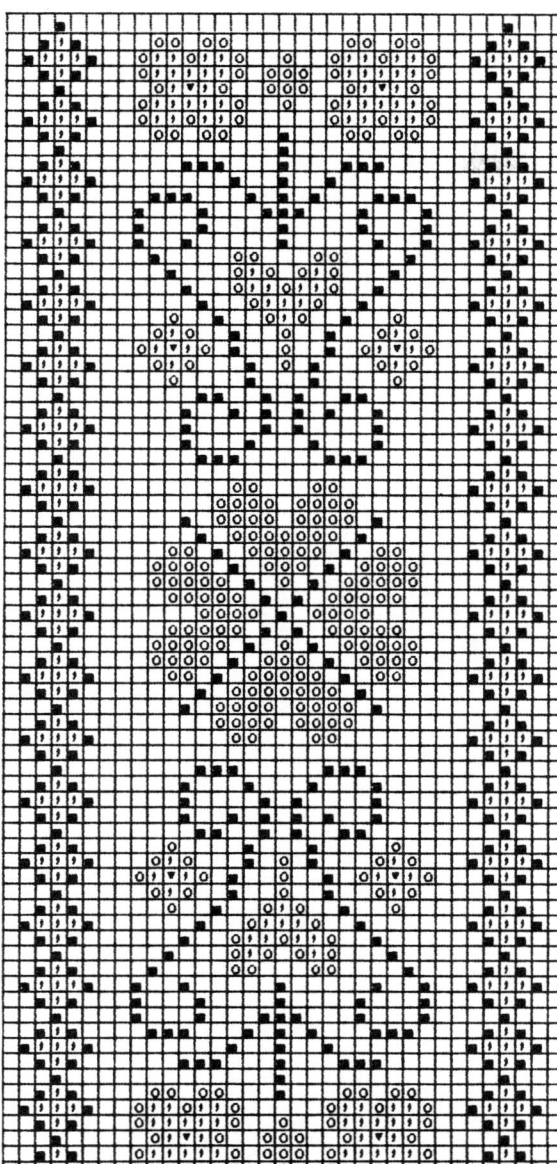

◄ DMC #
- ◯ 309 deep rose
- ■ 367 dark pistachio green
- ❶ 776 medium pink

Width with border: 33 squares
Width without border: 19 squares
Design length: 75 squares
Repeat length: 75 squares

► DMC #
- ▼ 824 very dark blue
- ◯ 826 medium blue
- ❶ 828 very pale blue
- ■ 987 medium forest green

Width with border: 31 squares
Width without border: 15 squares
Design length: 67 squares
Repeat length: 67 squares

▲	DMC #	
■	517	medium Wedgwood blue
O	519	sky blue
⁀	747	very light sky blue

Width with border: 47 squares
Width without border: 35 squares
Design length: 95 squares
Repeat length: 68 squares

▶	DMC #	
⁀	727	very light topaz
O	813	light blue
▼	825	dark blue

Width with border: 25 squares
Width without border: 11 squares
Design length: 29 squares
Repeat length: 32 squares

▲   DMC #
▼   312   light navy blue
◉   3325   baby blue

Width with border: 39 squares
Width without border: 31 squares
Design length: 93 squares
Repeat length: 72 squares

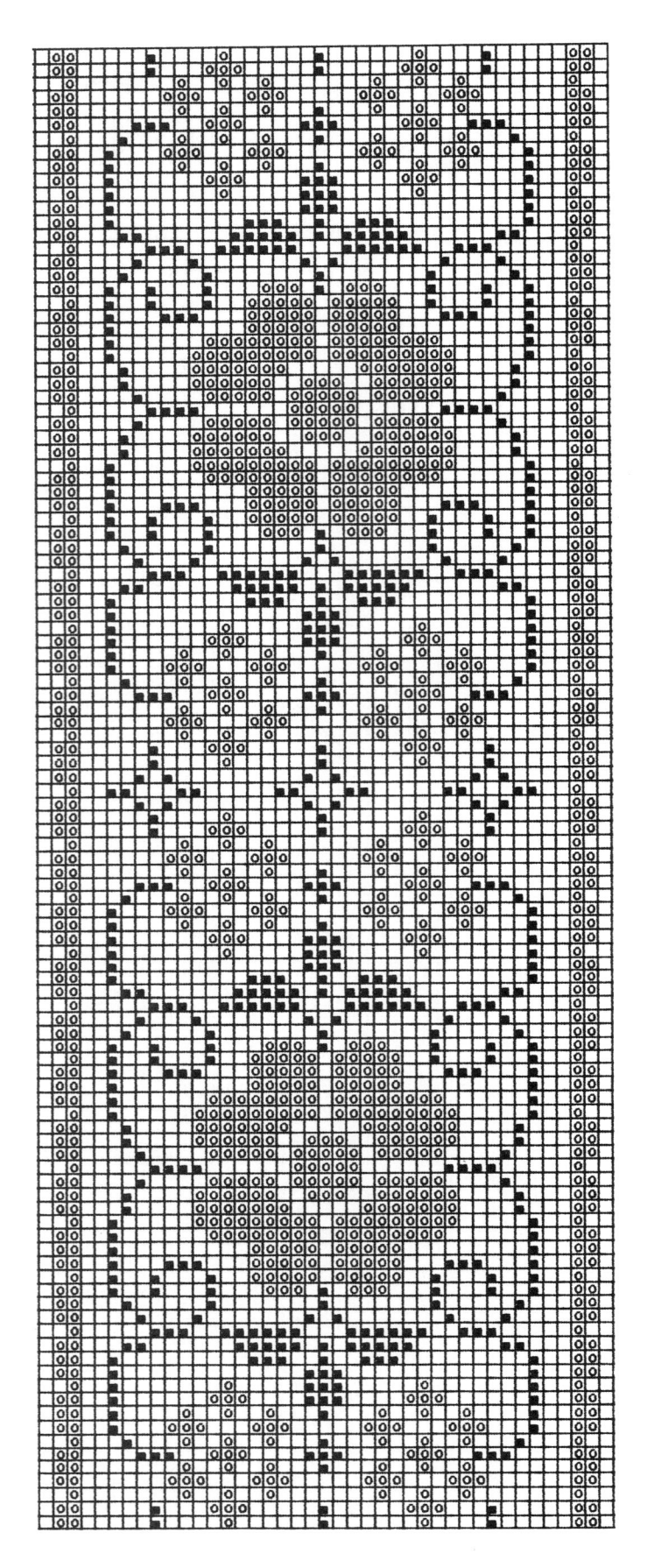

DMC #

- ■ 367 dark pistachio green
- ◉ 899 medium rose

Width with border: 39 squares
Width without border: 31 squares
Design length: 63 squares
Repeat length: 56 squares

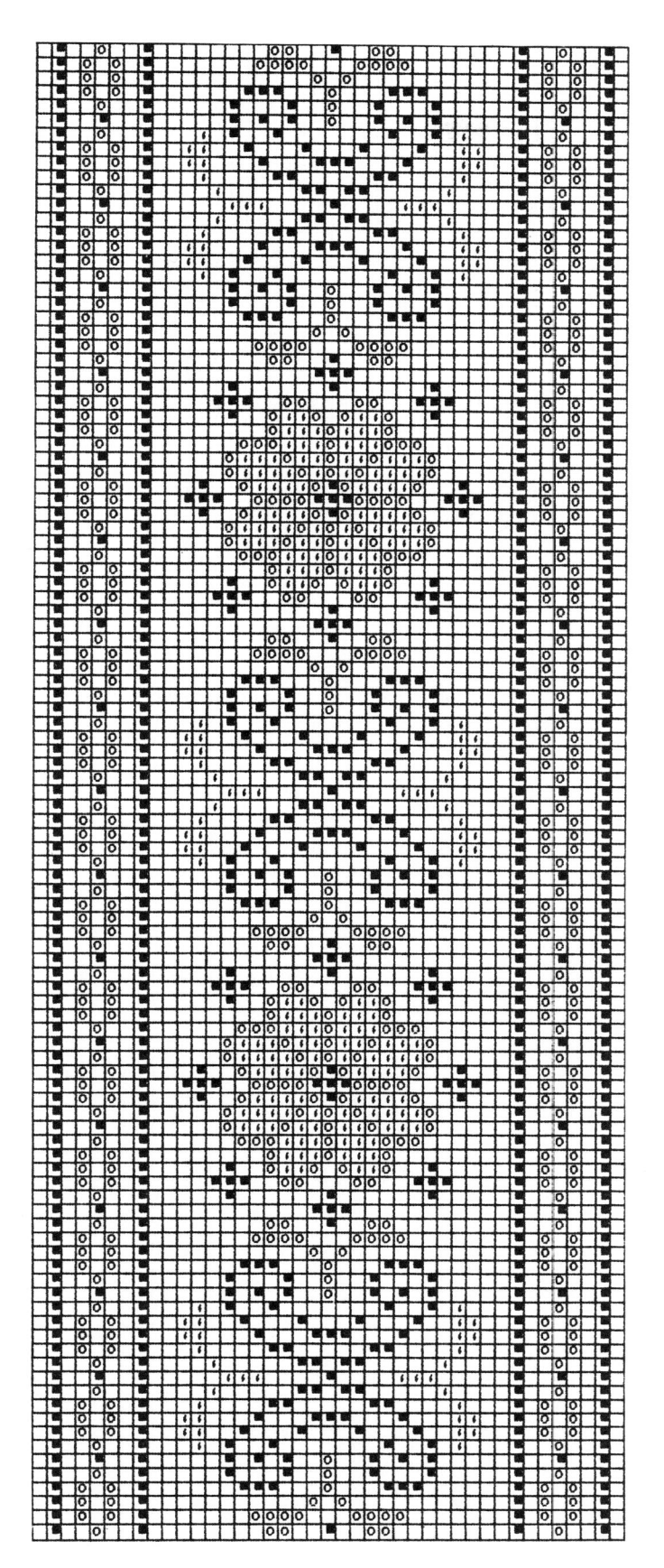

DMC #

■	517	medium Wedgwood blue
O	519	sky blue
?	747	very light sky blue

Width with border: 39 squares
Width without border: 21 squares
Design length: 65 squares
Repeat length: 42 squares

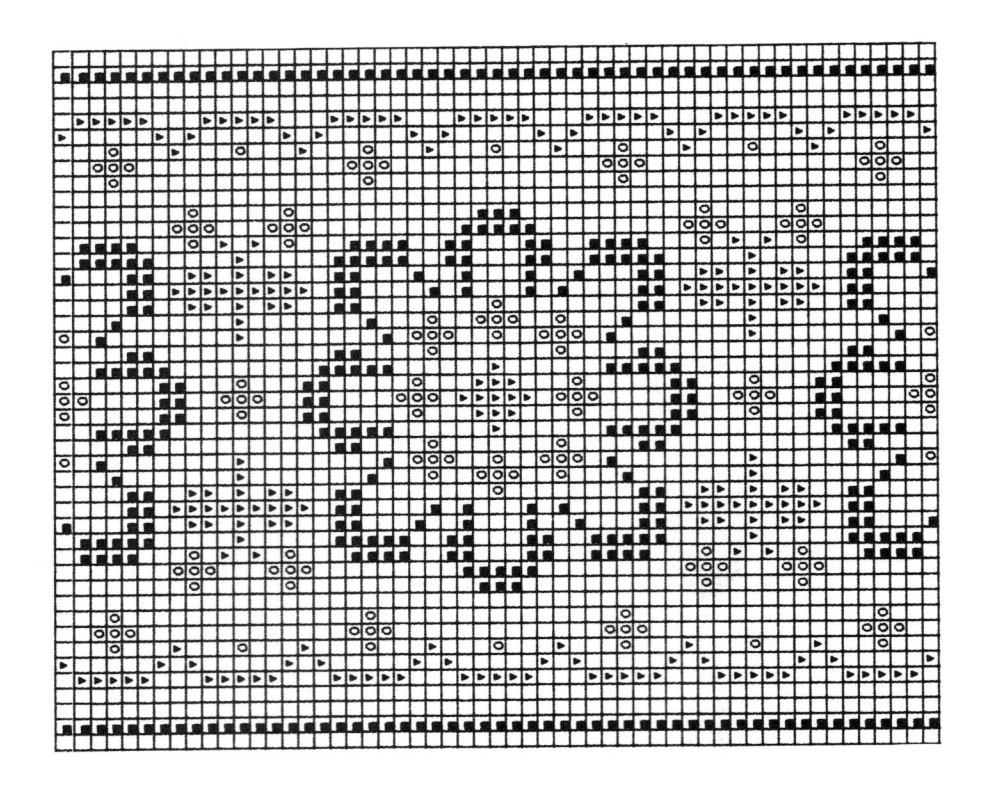

▲	DMC #		▼	DMC #	
■	311	medium navy blue	○	335	rose
▶	334	medium marine blue	■	367	dark pistachio green
○	775	light baby blue	▶	436	tan
			⌐	726	light topaz

Width with border: 43 squares
Width without border: 25 squares
Design length: 41 squares
Repeat length: 32 squares

Width with border: 43 squares
Width without border: 33 squares
Design length: 45 squares
Repeat length: 59 squares

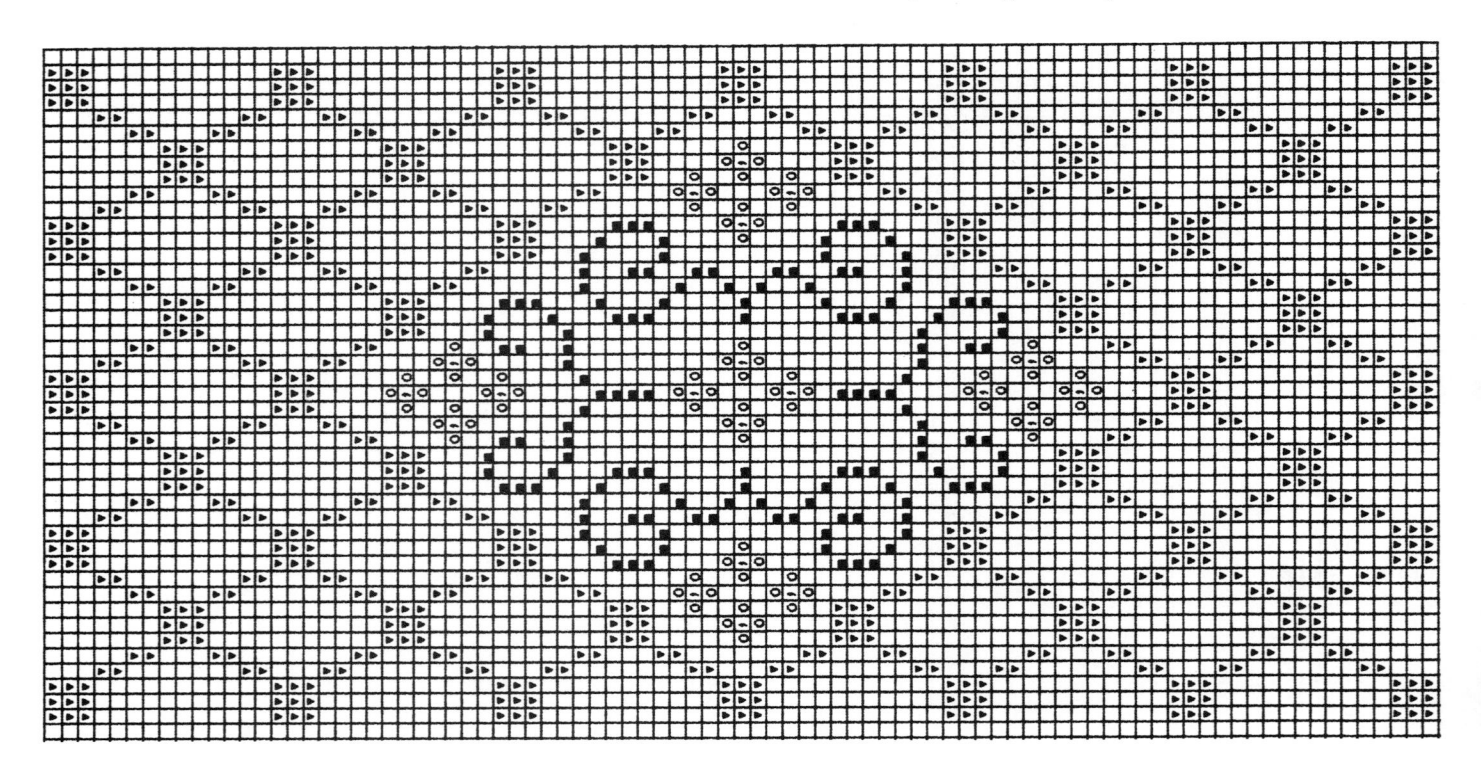

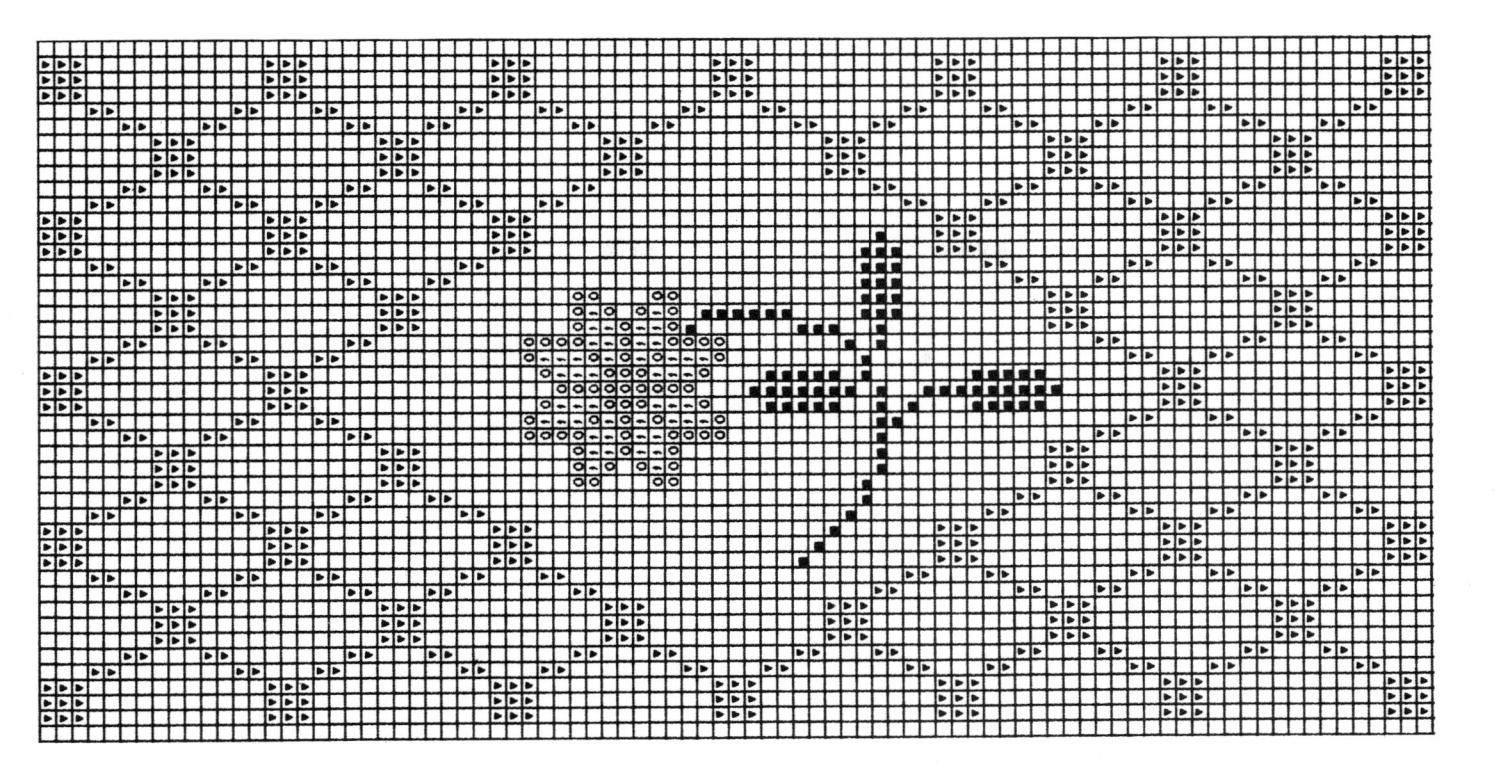

	DMC #	
○	309	deep rose
▶	436	tan
⌐	776	medium pink
■	987	medium forest green

Width with border: 43 squares
Width without border: 22 squares
Design length: 34 squares
Repeat length: 59 squares

	DMC #	
■	367	dark pistachio green
▶	436	tan
○	961	dark dusty rose

Width with border: 43 squares
Width without border: 31 squares
Design length: 39 squares
Repeat length: 59 squares

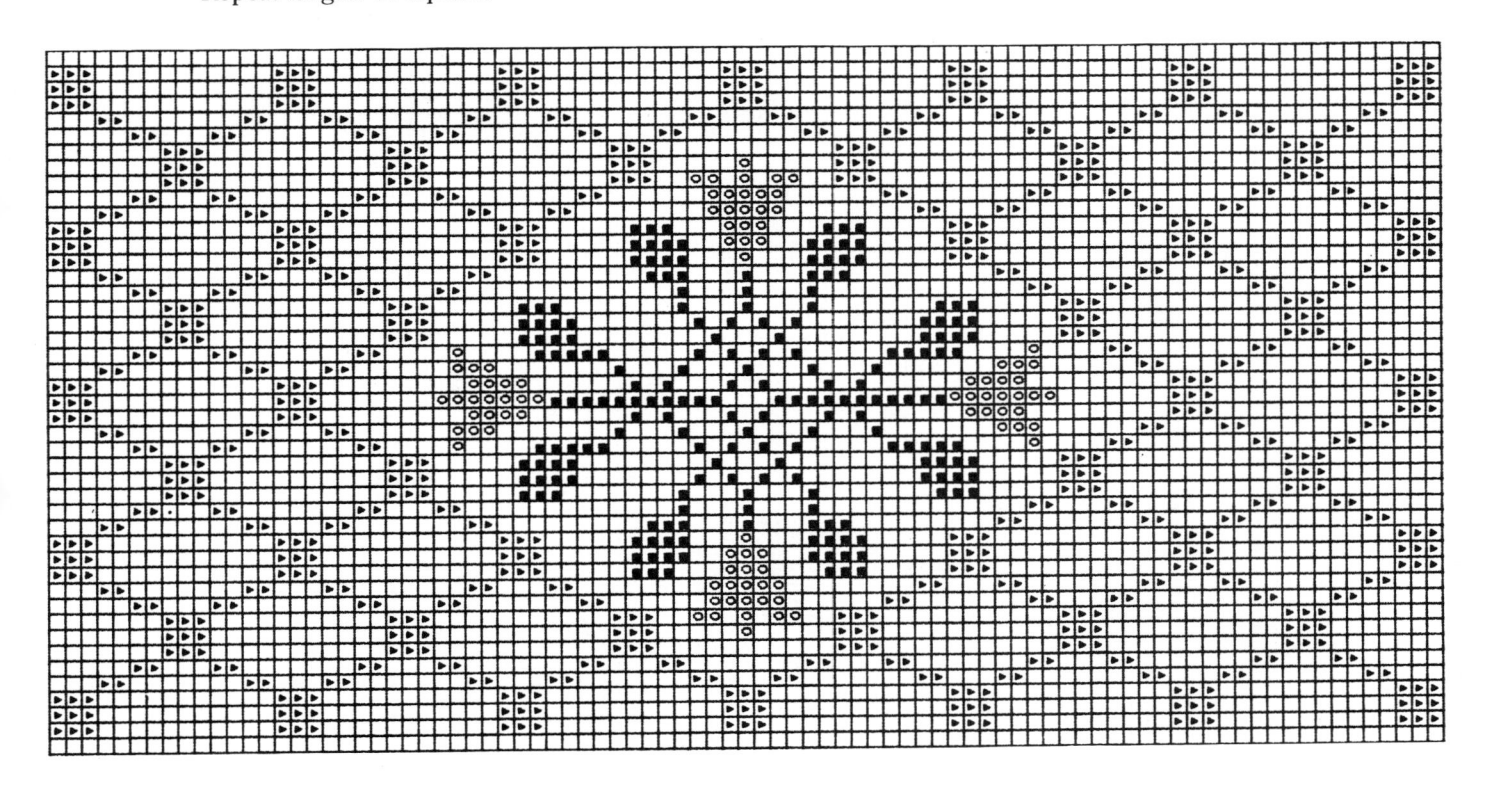

41

DMC #		
■	987	medium forest green
⌐	3078	very light golden yellow
▼	3350	very dark dusty rose
○	3354	light dusty rose

Width with border: 59 squares
Width without border: 45 squares
Design length: 125 squares
Repeat length: 80 squares

Width with border: 52 squares
Width without border: 32 squares
Design length: 71 squares
Repeat length: 48 squares

DMC #
■ 347 dark salmon
○ 838 very dark beige brown
▼ 842 very light beige brown

▼   *DMC #*
▼   813   light blue
■   824   very dark blue
◘   828   very pale blue

Width with border: 33 squares
Width without border: 23 squares
Design length: 43 squares
Repeat length: 30 squares

▲   *DMC #*
◘   312   light navy blue
▼   3325   baby blue

Width with border: 39 squares
Width without border: 31 squares
Design length: 31 squares
Repeat length: 24 squares

▲ DMC #
▲ 987 medium forest green
o 3350 very dark dusty rose
⁊ 3354 light dusty rose

Width with border: 31 squares
Width without border: 21 squares
Design length: 35 squares
Repeat length: 28 squares

▼ DMC #
o 604 light cranberry
▼ 954 Nile green

Width with border: 37 squares
Width without border: 23 squares
Design length: 23 squares
Repeat length: 30 squares

Width with border: 41 squares
Width without border: 33 squares
Design length: 31 squares
Repeat length: 34 squares

DMC #	
326	very deep rose
367	dark pistachio green
3326	light rose

DMC #
666　bright Christmas red
699　Christmas green
796　dark royal blue

Width with border: 61 squares
Width without border: 49 squares
Design length: 49 squares
Repeat length: 49 squares

DMC #
973　bright canary yellow
3345　dark hunter green

Width with border: 61 squares
Width without border: 39 squares
Design length: 45 squares
Repeat length: 29 squares

47

	DMC #	
◙	826	medium blue

Width with border: 67 squares
Width without border: 45 squares
Design length: 103 squares
Repeat length: 80 squares